Sun-Kissed
Quilts & Crafts

Create Original Sun-Printed Designs
on Fabric, Paper & More

Barbara K. Baker
& Jeri Boe

Text© 2005 Barbara K. Baker and Jeri Boe

Artwork © 2005 C&T Publishing, Inc.

Publisher: Amy Marson

Editorial Director: Gailen Runge

Acquisitions Editor: Jan Grigsby

Editor: Cyndy Lyle Rymer

Technical Editor: Gayl Gallagher

Copyeditor/Proofreader: Wordfirm Inc.

Cover Designer: Kristy K. Zacharias

Design Director/Book Designer: Kristy K. Zacharias

Illustrator: Kirstie McCormick

Production Assistant: Tim Manibusan

Photography: Diane Pedersen and Luke Mulks

Published by C&T Publishing, Inc., P.O. Box 1456, Lafayette, CA
  94549

Front cover: *Bubblicious* (page 31)

Back cover: *Aqua Blue Welcome* (page 49), *Sun-Printed Cards*.

Library of Congress Cataloging-in-Publication Data

Baker, Barbara K. (Barbara Kearney),
  Sun-kissed quilts & crafts : create original designs on fabric,
paper & more / Barbara K. Baker, Jeri Boe.
    p. cm.
  ISBN 1-57120-298-6 (paper trade)
  1. Textile painting. I. Boe, Jeri II. Title.
  TT851.B343 2005
  746.46'041—dc22
                    2004030314

Printed in Singapore

10 9 8 7 6 5 4 3 2 1

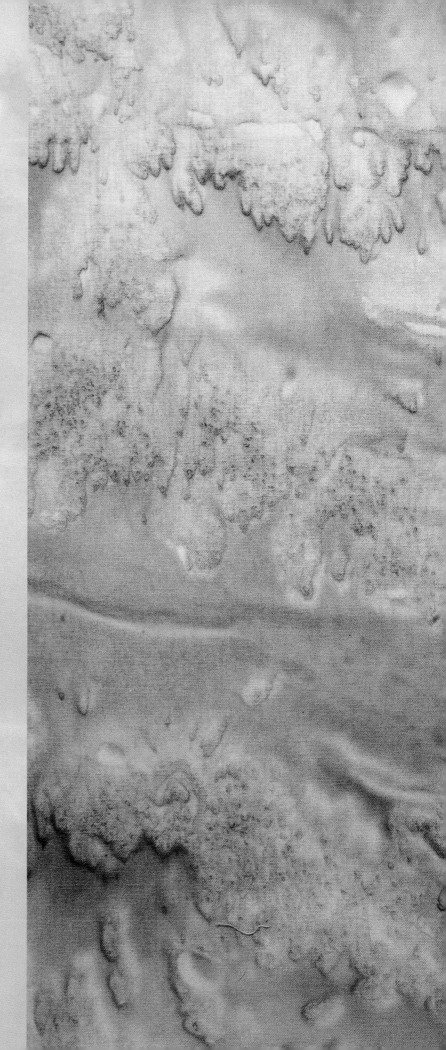

Dedication

We dedicate this book to all the people who love to have fun creating.

Acknowledgments

We would like to thank the following people:

The sun printing ladies who inspired us to write this book.

Everyone at C&T Publishing-you are all wonderful and a delight to work with.

To all of our Binding Angels: Sally Names, Virginia Mohr, Judy Ballew, Lorene Bateman, and Lee Greene. We couldn't have finished on time without you.

Special thanks go out to Jeri's sister, Sandi Ross, who tested the sun printing methods in this book.

We would also like to thank our families for giving us their support, garage, and driveway space for our sun printing adventures!

And finally, many thanks to the American Professional Quilting Systems for all their help and expertise with Barbara's longarm quilting machine. Quilting with her longarm has allowed Barbara to exercise her creativity in design and technique.

Contents

Preface

All you need to sun print successfully is a playful attitude. Sun printing doesn't require you to have any experience as a painter or any artistic talent at all. It does not require a sewing machine. Nontoxic paints are used, so almost anyone can enjoy this technique. Once you begin sun printing, you will realize how fun and easy the process truly is. Soon, people around you will want to sun print. Jeri's teenage daughter loves to sun print, and Jeri's husband is always bringing home "treasures" for Jeri to sun print.

Just What Is Sun Printing?

Sun printing, also known as sun painting or heliographic art, is a process in which light sensitive paints, such as Pebeo Setacolors, are applied to fabric (or other suitable materials). While the paint is still wet, objects like leaves, flowers, feathers, or cutouts are placed onto the wet fabric. Next, the fabric is placed in a sunny area or under another light source. The paint reacts to the light, and any area of the fabric exposed to the sun becomes printed. The area under the object and not exposed to light becomes pastel.

Origins of Sun Printing

Sun printing was "discovered" by artists on a Pacific island. A palm branch had accidentally fallen on a piece of freshly painted, wet fabric that had been left out in the sun to dry. When they removed the branch, a beautiful pastel image of the palm leaves was printed on the colorful fabric.

Jeri began experimenting with sun printing many years ago, after reading about the process in a book. Soon thereafter, Barbara joined her on the creative adventure. The more they sun printed, the more they were intrigued by it. Then they began teaching others. They started sharing sun printing with their family and friends, and soon grandmothers were spending the day sun printing with their grandchildren. What fun!

Once you start sun printing, ideas will begin to flow. You'll start thinking, "What if I did this?" or "I should try that!" You do not have complete control of the process, so each sun print is a unique work of art. Because sun printing requires input from nature, there is some unpredictability involved. Expect surprises!

The following chapters describe each step of sun printing, including helpful hints and lots of easy, fun suggestions. Be sure to read the entire Sun-Printing Techniques chapter before you start printing. This book also provides great ideas for how to use your beautiful fabric creations, as well as some fast and easy no-sew projects. So, put on some old clothes or a painting shirt, and prepare to have fun! We hope you enjoy the creative process of sun printing as much as we do.

Sun-Printing
TECHNIQUES

The Process
Sun printing is easy, fast, and fun for all ages. You do not need to know how to paint or sew. You don't even need to own a sewing machine! The basic supplies are simple and easy to find.

There are a few basic steps for creating a sun print. Some steps are described in more detail later in this chapter.

1. Test the paint on a corner of the fabric to make sure the fabric will accept the paint.

2. Decide what objects you want to sun print. Flat objects work the best, but dimensional objects may add a unique look.

3. Secure the fabric onto a board, or other surface, covered with plastic.

4. Prepare the paint wash.

5. Mist the fabric with water from a clean spray bottle, then apply the paint.

6. Place the objects to be sun printed on top of the wet, painted fabric, and carefully push or pin the objects as flat as possible against the fabric.

7. Place the fabric in the sun or under an artificial light source.

8. When the fabric is dry, remove the sun-printed objects.

9. To heat set the paints, simply iron the fabric for about 3 minutes on the cotton setting (or a setting appropriate for the fabric used) using a steady back and forth motion.

Sun-printed fabric is machine washable (no bleach) and can be dry-cleaned. The result is a one-of-a-kind piece of artwork!

tip

Sun printing is a great project for children, provided an adult supervises. An adult should do all of the ironing.

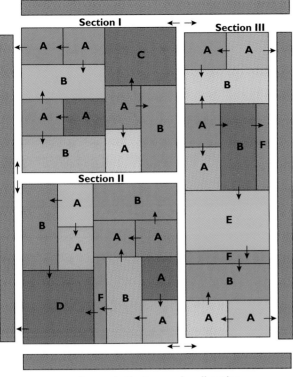

Arrows indicate pressing direction.

Quilt Assembly Diagram

- Machine trapunto some of the scenes if you have time.

- Add colored details with fabric markers. Color the leaves and flower centers. Then outline the shapes with a black fabric marker.

Embellishments

tip Use paints to add colors to the bubbles. Try Pebeo gold or pearl white to add shimmer. Then try some of the Pebeo Shimmer colors to make the bubbles glow.

Once you have assembled your quilt top, the fun begins.

- Choose decorative threads that match your block colors, and stitch away.

- Add dimension to the bubbles by stitching around the outer edge.

- Try some metallic threads to add some shimmer to the bubbles.

- Outline the leaves, flowers, and birds with decorative threads.

- Try couching on some heavier threads for interest.

- Sew beads in the flower centers for added dimension.

Finishing

1. Layer the backing, batting, and quilt top; baste.

2. Enhance your embellishments with decorative quilting. Stitch closely to the machine trapunto to make it lift up. Add leaves for the flower petals and swirling lines around the bubbles. Just enjoy yourself and create.

3. Attach a hanging sleeve if necessary.

4. Bind or finish as desired.

5. Attach a label.

tip Save those scraps of sun-printed fabric to make quick decorative gift bags.

Other Ideas

COMPOSITION IN BLUE
13½" x 13½", Hadi Sales, Redmond, Oregon, 2004

- Randomly make cuts in a sun-printed panel, then sew 1" strips between the cuts. Embellish with beads and quilting for an easy and beautiful mini-wallhanging.

FOREST FERN LINGERIE BAG
Jeri Boe, Bend, Oregon, 2004

- Make a beautiful lingerie bag (or purse) with your sun-printed panels.

SITTING PRETTY
Jeri Boe, Bend, Oregon, 2004

- A white director's chair is a quick and easy sun-printed accent for any room.

Maple Leaves

Need to add a little sparkle to your table? Let this Maple Leaves table runner grace your table. Create this one-of-a-kind centerpiece in a weekend, from start to finish.

tip

Try using a variety of leaves from your garden. Oak and aspen leaves or pine needles all create wonderful seasonal patterns. Don't forget those pesky grasses and weeds that hang out in the garden—they will create some wonderful designs.

Materials

Allow extra fabric for directional prints.

GOLD: ⅓ yard

LIGHT BLUE: ½ yard

DARK BLUE: ¼ yard

BINDING: ½ yard

BATTING: 22″ x 40″

BACKING: 1 yard

THREADS FOR EMBELLISHMENT

Cutting

GOLD

- Cut 3 strips 1½″ x the width of the fabric. Then cut into 4 H's 1½″ x 1½″ for the inner border, 2 K's 1½″ x 16½″, and 2 J's 1½″ x 34½″ for the outer border.
- Cut 1 strip 2½″ x the width of the fabric. Then cut into 2 B's 2½″ x 2½″ for the blocks and 1 E 2½″ x 16½″ for the top.
- Cut 4 C's 3½″ x 3½″ for the blocks.

LIGHT BLUE

- Cut 2 strips 6½″ wide, then cut 2 F's 6½″ x 24½″ for the top.
- Cut 4 A's 2½″ x 3½″ for the blocks.
- Cut 4 D's 3½″ x 5½″ for the blocks.

DARK BLUE

- Cut 3 strips 1½″ x the width of the fabric. Then cut into 4 L's 1½″ x 1½″ for the outer border and 2 I's 1½″ x 14½″ and 2 G's 1½″ x 32½″ for the inner border.

BINDING: Cut 3 strips 2½″ x the width of the fabric.

Block Assembly

1. Sew 1 blue rectangle A to 1 gold square B. Press to the dark. Make 2 units.

2. Sew 1 blue rectangle A to 1 gold square C. Press seams to the dark. Make 2 units.

3. Sew 2 blue/gold units together, following the diagram. Nest the seams. Make 2 units.

4. Twist the center seam open. Then press the seam to the gold.

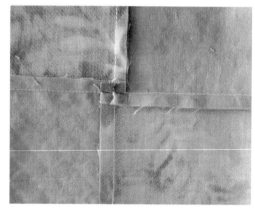

Twist seams.

5. Sew 1 blue rectangle D strip to the blue/gold unit to make Unit I. Press the seam to the blue. Make 2. Set aside.

6. Sew 1 gold square C to 1 blue rectangle D to make Unit II. Press the seam to the gold. Make 2.

7. Sew a Unit I to a Unit II to make a corner block. Twist the seams to lie flat. Press. Make 2.

 tip Make matching no-sew napkins to complement the table runner.

Table Runner Assembly

1. Sew the gold rectangle E to 1 blue rectangle F, stopping ½" from the end of the seam to create a partial seam. Press the seam to the gold.

2. Sew 1 block to top of this unit. Press the seam away from the block.

3. Sew remaining blue rectangle F to left side of the unit. Press the seam to the gold rectangle.

4. Fold the blue rectangle away from the partial seam. Sew the remaining block to the blue/gold unit. Press the seam away from the block.

5. Complete the partial seam. Match the remaining blue rectangle seam allowance to the block unit. Sew the seam. Press the seam toward the block.

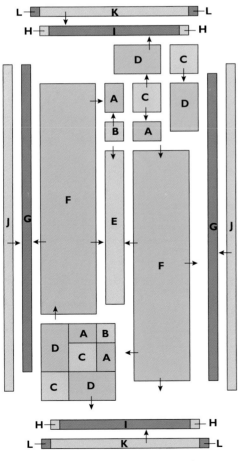

Arrows indicate pressing direction.

Quilt Assembly Diagram

BORDERS

1. Add a blue border strip G to each side of the quilt top. Press the seam to the border.

2. Sew 1 gold square H to each end of 1 blue rectangle I. Press to the dark. Make 2.

3. Sew 1 unit to the top and bottom of the quilt top. Press the seam toward the border.

4. Sew a gold border strip J to each side of the quilt top. Press the seam toward the blue border.

5. Sew dark blue squares L to each end of the gold strips K. Press to the blue. Make 2.

6. Sew 1 unit to the top and bottom of the quilt top. Press to the blue.

Finishing

1. Embellish the table runner with decorative threads by *outlining* the sun-printed shapes with rayon or metallic threads. Try adding leaves and tendrils in the open areas, or simply add some cross-hatching.

2. Layer the backing, batting, and quilt top; baste.

3. Quilt as desired to further enhance your designs.

4. Bind or finish as desired.

5. Attach a label.

tip

Add decorative beads, buttons, and threads to the table runner for sparkle and interest. Cluster them together to make a decorative flower or seed pod.

Embroider designs onto your sun-printed panels, then sew the top together for a quick holiday wallhanging.

Stencil or stamp leaf designs in colors that complement the table runner. Try gold or silver opaque paints for a holiday look.

Other Ideas

Use your sun-printed blocks as backgrounds for embroidery.

TRICK OR TREAT
29½" x 34", Barbara Baker, Bend, Oregon, 2004

■ Barbara used embroidery cards to create this quick quilt.

ARLO IN THE GRAPE ARBOR
32" x 47", Cyndy Lyle Rymer, Danville, California, 2004

■ Cyndy used freezer paper masks, narrow leaves, bone-shaped biscuits, and grape leaves to sun print the center panel and borders in this colorful pet quilt.

Spring Leaves Quilt

FINISHED SIZE: 48" x 48"

Soft yellows, greens, reds, oranges, and blues evoke tender new leaves and spring flowers. Gather your leaves, ferns, and flower petals to create this sun print on a warm spring day.

tip

Visit your local florist to find unique leaves and flowers. A small bouquet will have just the right mix of ferns and flowers, even some exotic flowers and leaves.

Materials

Allow extra fabric for directional prints.

AQUA: 1⅓ yard

BLUE: 1 yard

YELLOW: ⅝ yard

SPRING GREEN: ⅔ yard

RED: ¾ yard

ORANGE: ¼ yard

BINDING: ⅜ yard

BACKING: 3 yards

BATTING: 52″ x 52″

PAPER-BACKED FUSIBLE WEB:
1 yard

**LIGHTWEIGHT, WATER-SOLUBLE STABILIZER
(SUCH AS SULKY SOLVY):**
2 yards

THREADS TO MATCH

METALLIC THREAD FOR ACCENT

Cutting

QUILT TOP PIECES

AQUA

- Cut 1 P 1½″ x 44½″ for the top sashing.
- Cut 1 G 21¼″ x 18½″ for Section II.
- Cut 1 O 4¼″ x 21¼″ for Section III.
- Cut 1 A 5″ x 21¾″ for Section I.
- Cut 1 J 3½″ x 9½″.
- Cut 1 K 3½″ x 23″

BLUE

- Cut 1 I 3½″ x 14″ for Section IV.
- Cut 1 L 17¾″ x 23″ for Section IV.

YELLOW

- Cut 1 B 1½″ x 5″ for Section I.
- Cut 1 D 3½″ x 19¾″ for Section I.
- Cut 1 strip 3½″ wide. Then cut into 1 E 3½″ x 16½″ for Section I and 1 M 3½″ x 18¼″ for Section III.
- Cut 1 H 4″ x 21¼″ for Section II.

SPRING GREEN

- Cut 1 F 1½″ x 21″ for Section I.
- Cut 1 C 19¾″ x 13½″ for Section I.
- Cut 1 N 18¼″ x 18¼″ for Section III.

RED

- Cut 5 strips 2½″ wide. Sew into 1 long strip, then cut into 2 Q's 2½″ x 44½″ and 2 R's 2½″ x 48½″ for the border.

APPLIQUÉ

AQUA

- Cut 1 AA 3½″ x 5½″, 1 BB 3½″ x 3½″, and 1 CC 6″x 6″.

BLUE

- Cut 1 EE 4½″ x 8½″ for Section II.
- Cut 1 DD 6″ x 6″ for Section I, 1 HH 6″ x 7″ for Section IV, and 1 GG 6″ x 7½″ for Section III.
- Cut 1 FF 6½″ x 6½″ for the center.

YELLOW

- Cut 1 II 8″ x 7½″ for Section I.
- Cut 1 JJ 6½″ x 6″ for Section II.
- Cut 1 KK 5½″ x 8½″.
- Cut 1 LL 8½″ x 7½″ for the center.
- Cut 1 MM 5″x 4½″ for Section III, and 1 NN 5″ x 7½″ for Section IV.

BINDING: Cut 5 strips 2½″ wide x the width of the fabric.

RED

- Cut 1 SS 3½" x 5" for Section IV.
- Cut 1 OO 4½" x 7" for Section I.
- Cut 1 strip 5½" wide. Then cut into 1 PP and 1 RR 5½" x 5½" for Section II and III.
- Cut 1 QQ 8½" x 5½" for the center.

ORANGE

- Cut 1 TT 3½" x 4½" for Section I.
- Cut 1 WW 3½" x 4½" for Section IV and 1 VV 5½" x 5½" for the center.
- Cut 1 UU 6" x 3" for Section II, and 1 XX 5½" x 3½" for Section III.

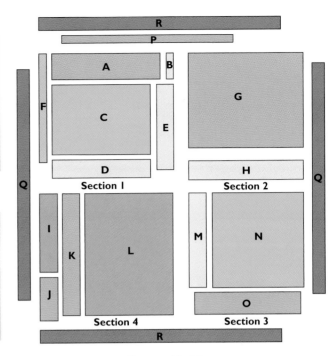

Quilt Assembly Diagram

Quilt Assembly

1. Lay out the fabric pieces as shown in the Quilt Assembly Diagram.

2. Sew all the pieces for Section I together. Press all seams to the darker fabric.

3. Sew all the pieces for Section II, III, and IV together in the same manner.

4. Sew Section I to Section IV. Press the seam open.

5. Sew Section II to Section III. Press the seam open.

6. Sew Section I/IV to Section II/II. Press the seam open.

7. Sew sashing (P) to the quilt top.

8. Add the red side borders, then the top and bottom borders. Press all seams toward the borders.

Appliqué

1. Trace the appliqué shapes to the paper side of the paper-backed fusible web. Cut the shapes from the paper-backed fusible web and iron to the back side of the appliqué pieces, following the manufacturer's instructions.

2. Lay out the appliqué pieces on the quilt top as shown on page 42. Arrange the pieces until you have a pleasing arrangement, then fuse in place.

3. Pin the stabilizer to the wrong side of the quilt top.

4. Fill the bobbin with a lightweight thread. Loosen the top tension, and choose a decorative stitch to appliqué your piece.

5. Machine appliqué around the edges.

6. When you have completed your stitching, cut away the excess stabilizer and save it for future projects. Immerse the quilt top in warm water to remove the rest of the stabilizer. Press dry.

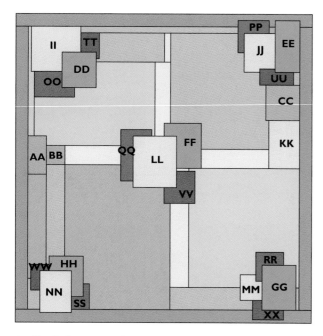

Appliqué Placement Diagram

tip Try adding different appliqué shapes, such as circles, ovals, or diamonds to the quilt top.

tip Create dragonfly wings! Save all those threads scraps. Layer them between two layers of water-soluble stabilizer, then stitch together with a decorative thread, catching all the threads together. Wash out the stabilizer, then attach the wings to your quilt top for a one-of-a-kind embellishment!

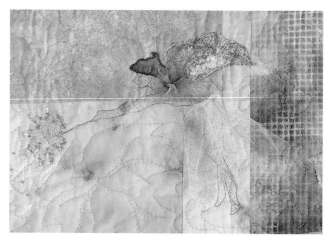

Create a sweet fairy...

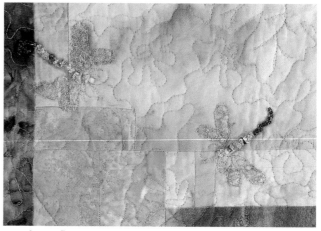

or a dragonfly or two.

Finishing

1. Layer the backing, batting, and top; baste or pin in place.

2. We chose to highlight the leaves and ferns with decorative threads. Upon close inspection, you will see a fairy nestled among the ferns. Be creative and have fun with your quilting.

3. Attach a hanging sleeve, if necessary.

4. Bind or finish as desired.

5. Attach a label.

tip Use machine trapunto to make the fairy shape pop.

Other Ideas

MCKENZIE RIVER RENDEZVOUS
38" x 38", Jeri Boe, Bend, Oregon, 2004

▪ If you just can't cut into your panels, then collage them together to create a quilt.

PURPLE NELLIE
30" x 26", Sally Names, Bend, Oregon, 2004

▪ Attach decorative beads to create the dragonfly or flower centers. Then couch fancy yarns onto the flower petals.

SPARKLING LEAVES
33½" x 30", Carol Elsbree, Sunriver, Oregon, 2004

■ Try adding paints, metallic threads, bead embellishments, silk ribbon, or decorative quilting to embellish your prints.

MORNING MIST
34" x 26½", Judy Ballew, Bend, Oregon, 2004

Summer Sampler

FINISHED SIZE: 51½" x 45½"

This Summer Sampler is a play day just waiting to happen. Try every technique from this book, then start experimenting. Visit your kitchen cupboards for those curly macaroni pieces, try that wavy sink drain, and grab that carpet mesh.

tip

Try spiral or bow-tie macaroni for different shapes in your panels. Visit your local supermarket and specialty shops to find unique or seasonal macaroni shapes.

Materials

CENTER PANEL: 20″ x 17″

MULTICOLORED PANELS: 4 panels 18″ x 20″ (These panels should have the same colors as the center panel.)

BLACK: 1 yard

GOLD BORDER: ¼ yard

BLUE BORDER 1: ⅝ yard

BLUE BORDER 2: ⅜ yard

BLUE BORDER 3: ¼ yard

BINDING: ½ yard

BACKING: 3 yards

BATTING: 55″ x 49″

DECORATIVE THREADS TO MATCH

PAINTS TO EMBELLISH

Cutting

CENTER PANEL: Cut 1 rectangle 20″ x 17″.

MULTICOLORED PANELS: Refer to the color photo for the strip placement and color choices.

FOR SECTION I: Cut 1 strip 2″ x 8½″.

Cut 3 strips 4½″ x 8½″.

Cut 1 strip 8½″ x 8½″.

FOR SECTION II: Cut 1 strip 1½″ x 3½″.

Cut 1 strip 1½″ x 5″.

Cut 10 squares 2″ x 2″.

Cut 1 strip 4½″ x 5½″.

Cut 1 strip 4½″ x 8½″.

Cut 1 strip 5½″ x 14″.

SECTION III: Cut 1 strip 2″ x 4½″.

Cut 5 strips 4½″ x 4½″.

BLACK: Cut 11 strips 2½″ wide. Then cut 2 of the strips into 6 sashing strips 2½″ x 8½″ for Section I.

Cut 3 of the strips into 2 sashing strips 2½″ x 4½″, 1 sashing strip 2½″ x 5½″, and 4 sashing strips 2½″ x 20″ for Section II.

Cut 1 of the strips into 6 sashing strips 2½″ x 4½″ for Section III.

Cut 4 strips 2½″ x 34″ for the vertical sashing between the sections.

GOLD BORDER: Cut 2 strips 1½″ x 34″ and 2 strips 1½″ x 42½″.

BLUE OUTER BORDER 1: Cut 3 strips 5½″ wide. From these, cut 1 strip 5½″ x 9½″, 1 strip 5½″ x 12″, 1 strip 5½″ x 14½″, 1 strip 5½″ x 16½″, and 1 strip 5½″ x 42½″.

BLUE 2: Cut 1 strip 5½″ x 28½″ and 1 strip 5½″ x 34½″.

BLUE 3: Cut 1 strip 5½″ x 21″.

BINDING: Cut 5 strips 2½″ wide x the width of the fabric.

Quilt Assembly

1. Lay out all the fabric pieces as shown in the Quilt Assembly Diagram.

2. Sew all the pieces for Section I together. Press all seams to the black fabric. Set aside.

3. For Section II, pick a pleasing collection of 6 squares 2″ x 2″ and 1 strip 1½″ x 5″. Sew together as shown. Press according to the arrows.

4. For Section II, pick a pleasing collection of 4 squares 2″ x 2″ and 1 strip 1½″ x 3½″. Sew together as shown. Press according to the arrows.

5. Sew all pieces for Section II together. Press. Set aside.

6. For Section III, pick a pleasing 4½″ square to sew to the 2″ x 4½″ strip. Press the seam to the strip.

7. Sew all the remaining pieces for Section III together. Press.

8. Sew Section I to Section II. Press the seam open.

9. Sew Section I/II to Section III. Press the seam open.

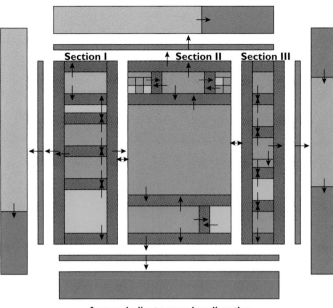

Arrows indicate pressing direction.

Quilt Assembly Diagram

BORDERS

1. Add the gold side borders, then the top and bottom borders. Press all seams toward the border.

2. Sew the 5½" x 42½" blue border 1 strip to the bottom of the quilt top. Press seam to the border.

3. For the top border, sew a 5½" x 14½" blue #1 strip to a 5½" x 28½" blue #2 strip. Press the seam. Sew the border to the quilt top.

4. For the left border, sew a 5½" x 12" blue #1 strip to a 5½" x 34½" blue #2 strip. Press the seam. Sew to the side of the quilt top. Press the seam to the border.

5. For the right border, sew a 5½" x 9½" blue #1 strip to a 5½" x 21" blue #3 strip, then add a 5½" x 16½" blue #1 strip. Press the seams. Sew to the side of the quilt top. Press the seam to the border.

tip Create a collage of colors. Randomly sew together pieces of your sun-printed scraps. Then cut the pieced fabrics to the sizes needed for the sampler pieces. You will be pleasantly surprised with the color and texture combinations.

Embellishments

■ Use decorative paints to add colors to some of the sun-printed areas.

■ Try some gold or silver colors to add sparkle to the quilt top.

■ Outline the painted shapes with a black fabric marker. Highlight the wings, eyes, and body shapes for the dragonfly. Add decorative shapes inside the body or wings for interest.

tip Use a metal-tipped applicator to apply a fine line of paint to the quilt top. Add free-hand decorative swirls, cross-hatching, stars, diamonds, and so on. The sky is the limit for embellishments.

Finishing

1. Layer the backing, batting, and quilt top; baste.

2. Quilting is the next step to finish your quilt top. Stitch wavy lines, cross-hatching, and grids to match the sun-printed shapes. Add flowers and leaves where the colors suggest a garden. Be creative with your quilting designs.

3. Attach a hanging sleeve, if necessary.

4. Bind or finish as desired.

5. Attach a label.

tip Create sun-printed labels for your quilts.

Other Ideas

UNDER THE SEA
54" x 50", Barbara Baker, Bend, Oregon, 2004

■ Scrunch sheer fabric for sun printing, then attach it to your quilt top to create undersea corals of all colors. Decorative yarns become seaweed, and beads become eyes for the seahorse and fish.

■ Add additional black sashing to create bed-size quilts using all your panels.

SUNPRINTING ADVENTURES
48" x 59", Pamela Mahn, LaPorte, Indiana, 2004

MEMORIES OF MOMMY
50½" x 46½", Krispi Staude, Friday Harbor, Washington, 2004

Aqua Blue Welcome

FINISHED SIZE: 18" x 49"

A welcome accent to grace any home, create this simple door knocker in a day with three sun-printed panels. Embellishments are the icing on the cake. Hang with a decorative rod or twig, and the piece is complete.

tip Change the colors and design panels to create a collection of seasonal door knockers to welcome your guests.

Materials

Allow extra fabric for directional prints.

AQUA: 2 panels 18" x 20"

PURPLE: 2 panels 18" x 20"

DARK PURPLE: ½ yard

BINDING: ½ yard

BACKING: 1 yard

BATTING: 22" x 53"

WROUGHT IRON OR WIRE HANGER

PAINTS

THREADS TO MATCH

Cutting

AQUA

- Cut 1 strip 2½" x 14" for the sashing.
- Cut 2 strips 2⅞" wide. Then cut into 9 squares 2⅞" x 2⅞" for the border.
- Cut 2 squares 14" x 14" for the top and bottom panels.

PURPLE

- Cut 2 strips 2½" wide. Then cut into 1 strip 2½" x 14" and 1 strip 2½" x 18" for the sashing.
- Cut 2 strips 2⅞" wide. Then cut into 9 squares 2⅞" x 2⅞" for the border.
- Cut 1 rectangle 12" x 14" for the center panel. panels.

DARK PURPLE

- Cut 1 strip 1⅞" wide. Then cut 1 strip 1⅞" x 10" and 1 strip 1⅞" x 12" for the bottom border.
- Cut 1 strip 2½" x 18" for the top border.
- Cut 2 strips 2⅞" wide. Then cut into 21 squares 2⅞" x 2⅞" for 2 flip-and-sew corners and 18 pairs of half-square triangles.

BINDING: Cut 4 strips 2½" wide x the width of the fabric.

Block Assembly

1. Make the half-square triangles by layering 9 aqua and 9 dark purple 2⅞" x 2⅞" squares, right sides together. Draw a diagonal line from corner to corner, and sew ¼" seam on each side of line. Cut apart on the drawn line, and press toward the dark. Trim off the dog-ears. You will end up with 18 half-square triangles. Set aside.

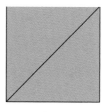

Draw a diagonal line.

Sew ¼" seam on each side of the line.

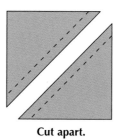

Cut apart.

2. Repeat Step 1 with 9 purple and 9 dark purple squares. Set aside.

Quilt Assembly

1. Lay out the 3 panels on a design wall.

2. Sew the purple 2½" x 14" strip to the lower edge of the top panel. Press the seam to the sashing strip. Set aside.

3. Sew the aqua 2½" x 14" strip to the lower edge of the center panel. Press the seam to the sashing strip. Set aside.

4. Fold the bottom panel in half lengthwise to find the center, and mark the center with a fine pencil. Measure down 8¼" from the top on each side of the panel, and mark with a fine pencil. Draw a diagonal line from each side to the center mark. Cut on the drawn line.

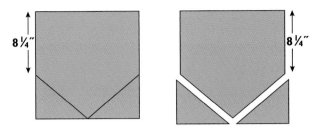

Draw diagonal lines, then cut on drawn lines.

5. Sew the top, center, and bottom panel units together. Set aside.

BORDERS

1. Following the color photo for placement, sew 18 half-square triangle units together to form each side border. There will be a left border and right border strip. Press seams open.

2. Cut 1 dark purple 2⅞" x 2⅞" square in half. Sew 1 triangle to the bottom end of each border strip. Press to the purple. Set aside.

3. Find the center point of the left side of the bottom border. Mark with a pin. Find the center mark of the 1⅞" x 10" dark purple strip; mark with a pin. Match the center pins, and sew the strip together. Press the seam to the purple. Trim off the excess purple strip.

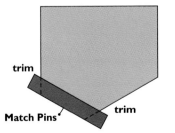

Match pins and sew. Trim off excess fabric.

4. For the right side of the bottom border, repeat Step 3 for the 1⅞" x 12" dark purple.

5. Sew the side borders onto the top. Press the seams away from the borders. Set aside.

6. Mark a diagonal line on the 2 dark purple 2⅞" x 2⅞" squares. Place 1 square on each end of the purple 2½" x 18" strip, right sides together.

7. Sew on the drawn line. Trim away the excess fabric. Press the triangle open, pressing the seam to the dark.

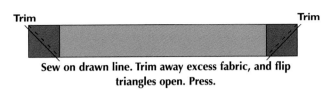

Sew on drawn line. Trim away excess fabric, and flip triangles open. Press.

8. Sew the dark purple 2½" x 18" strip to the top sashing strip. Refer to the Door Knocker Assembly for proper placement. Press the seam to the dark.

9. Sew this sashing unit to the top of the door knocker. Press the seam toward the sashing unit.

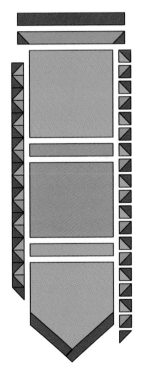

Door Knocker Assembly Diagram

tip Strapped for time? Use a complementary fabric for the border. Cut strips the size of the border measurements, then sew together.

Finishing

tip For a quick finish, instead of binding use the pillowcase technique. Place the quilt top and backing right sides together. Add the batting to the backing side. Stitch all 3 layers together, leaving a 3" opening at the edge for turning. Trim the batting close to the seam. Turn the piece right side out. Press, then whipstitch the opening closed. Quilt through all 3 layers.

1. Embellish the Door Knocker with paints, inks, threads, or buttons. Couch decorative threads to the designs for further interest.

2. Layer the backing, batting, and top; baste.

3. Quilt as desired.

4. Attach a hanging sleeve to the back of the door knocker.

5. Bind or finish as desired.

6. Attach a label.

tip Add decorative buttons to the quilt top in place of quilting. Sew the buttons in a random pattern or place them in the sashing.

Other Ideas

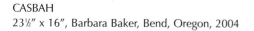
CASBAH
23½" x 16", Barbara Baker, Bend, Oregon, 2004

■ Sew a quick-and-easy table topper with one center panel. Add a satin-stitched swirl on each side, then some decorative beads and quilt as desired.

KING LEO
21½" x 21½", Barbara Baker, Bend, Oregon, 2004

■ Simply sew borders onto a panel, then embellish with inks, metallic paints, and beads to add color and sparkle.

Piecing Pi

FINISHED BLOCK SIZE: 8" x 8"
FINISHED QUILT SIZE: 35" x 35"

Have fun using sun prints with this easy, curved piecing project. Bubble wrap and grid overlays make this quilt a geometric wonder.

Materials

SUN-PRINTED PANELS: 6 or more panels 18" x 20"

DARK BLUE: ¼ yard for border 1

GRASS GREEN: ⅜ yard for border 2

BLUE PRINT: ⅜ yard for border 3

PURPLE PRINT: ⅜ yard for border 3

DARK GREEN: ¼ yard or scraps for corner border blocks

BINDING: ⅓ yard

BACKING: 1¼ yards

BATTING: 39" x 39"

Cutting

NOTE: Enlarge patterns A, B, and C 165% and add ¼" seam allowance to all pieces.

BLOCKS: Cut 9 each of patterns A, B, and C (see page 55).

tip Grainline is very important. Keep the grainlines running in the same direction, either lengthwise or crosswise.

Piece borders as necessary to obtain the correct lengths for the borders.

BORDER 1: Cut 2 strips 1¼" x 24½" and 2 strips 1¼" x 26½".

BORDER 2: Cut 2 strips 1¾" x 26½" and 2 strips 1¾" x 28½".

BLUE BORDER 3: Cut 2 strips 4" x 28½".

PURPLE BORDER 3: Cut 2 strips 4" x 28½".

CORNER BORDER BLOCKS: Cut 4 squares 4" x 4".

BINDING: Cut 4 strips 2" wide x the width of the fabric.

tip Try using different sizes of bubble wrap and carpet grids for these sun prints. Try putting the bubble wrap over or under the fabric.

Block Assembly

1. Pin the convex (outer) side of A to the concave (inner) side of B, marking and matching the centers of both pieces. Place the concave piece on top and the convex piece underneath. Pin from the center to each end, trying to keep an even distribution of fabric along the curve.

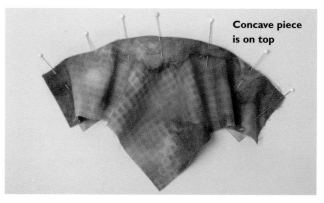

Concave piece is on top

Match and pin the pieces.

2. Shorten the stitch length on your sewing machine. With the concave piece on the top, stitch piece A to B using a ¼" seam allowance. Make sure there are no puckers in the seam. If there are any wrinkles in the seam allowance, make a small clip ⅛" from the stitching at the wrinkle.

Sew with the concave piece on top.

3. Sew the concave side of C to the convex side of the AB unit, following the same method as in Step 2. Square up the block to 8½" x 8½". Make 9 blocks.

4. Using a dry iron, press the AB unit from the right side of the block. Let the ruffles in the seam allowance lie naturally.

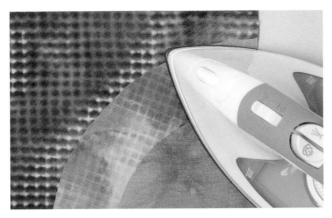
Press from the right side.

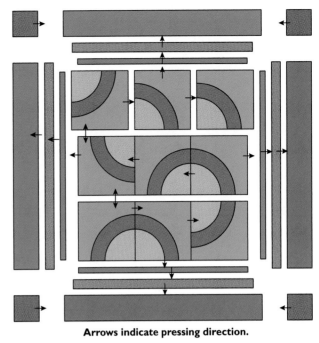
Arrows indicate pressing direction.
Quilt Assembly Diagram

Quilt Assembly

1. Following the Quilt Assembly Diagram and referring to the photo, stitch the blocks together in rows. Press as directed by the arrows.

2. Sew the rows together, and press as directed.

3. Sew border 1 to the top and bottom of the quilt top. Press toward the border. Attach border 1 sides to the quilt top, and press toward the border. Repeat for border 2.

4. Add border 3 top blue strip and bottom purple strip to the quilt top. Press toward the border.

5. Sew green 4″ x 4″ squares onto each end of the remaining border 3 pieces. Press toward the border.

6. Sew border 3 sides onto the quilt top. Press toward the borders.

Finishing

1. Layer the backing, batting, and quilt top; baste.

2. Quilt as desired.

3. Attach a hanging sleeve, if necessary.

4. Bind or finish as desired.

5. Attach a label.

tip Make 4 extra blocks, and use them to make a matching pillow.

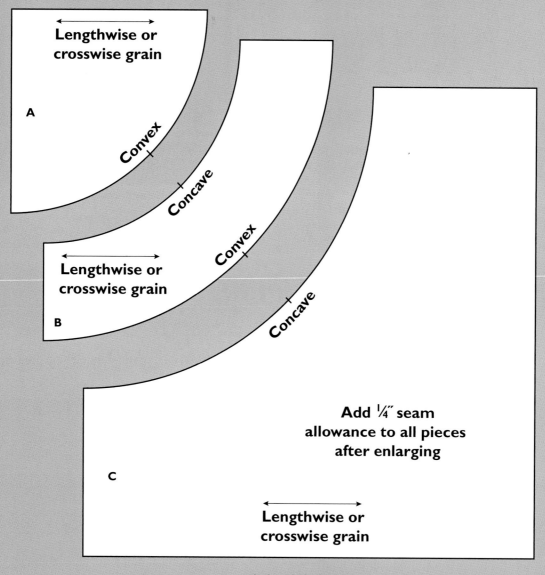

Lengthwise or crosswise grain

A

Convex

Concave

Lengthwise or crosswise grain

B

Convex

Concave

Add ¼″ seam allowance to all pieces after enlarging

C

Lengthwise or crosswise grain

Piecing Pi Block Patterns

Enlarge pattern pieces 165%.

Other Ideas

SUNSET GARDEN
32" x 33", Lorene Bateman, Bend, Oregon, 2004

■ Create a quilt using four sun-printed panels. Then sun print a complementary border to blend the quilt together.

SUN TEA TIME
20" x 29", Virginia Mohr, Bend, Oregon, 2004

■ Paper piece a collection of teapot, cups, and saucers for a cheerful wallhanging. Don't forget to add your cookies to the quilt top.

STARS TO DYE FOR
15" x 15", Loretta Smith, Bend, Oregon, 2004

■ Save all those little sun-printed scraps to create this
miniature star quilt. Add a decorative vine, then appliqué
flowers on top to finish the piece.

No-Sew PROJECTS

No-sew projects are truly fast, easy, and fun. They satisfy our cravings for instant gratification and make great projects for children as well as adults. All ages love to experience the magic of sun printing and enjoy the satisfaction of finishing a project quickly. Just follow a few tips for success, and allow the creativity to flow.

Selection Guidelines

You can sun print many different items. The best way to discover a new item is to walk around a store and look for white or light-colored items made from fabric. If it is 100% cotton, silk, or rayon, then consider it for sun printing. Terry cloth and other high-nap fabrics do not sun print well. Make sure the item does not have a special coating that will prevent the absorption of paint. Evaluate the object. If it will lie flat, then it will be easy to sun print. If it is dimensional, then it will be more challenging to keep the masks in place.

Start by practicing on single-sided items that lie flat, such as bandanas or napkins. Once you understand how the paint flows, move onto small, double-sided items, like gift bags.

tip
Create matching tablecloths and napkins with sun printing.

Single-Sided, Ready-Made Items

Single-sided items—bandanas, napkins, tablecloths, aprons, sheets, scarves, and so on—are the easiest items to sun print. Simply sun print the item using the same method as you would for fabric (pages 11–16).

Double-Sided, Ready-Made Items

Double-sided items—such as gift bags, T-shirts, baby cover-ups, and tote bags—are great for sun printing. Just print one side at a time.

1. To prevent the paint from flowing through to the other side, place lightweight plastic between the layers of the object.

2. Lightly moisten only the area you plan to paint, to prevent unwanted wicking of water and paint.

3. Allow 1 side to completely dry before working on the other side.

Other Ideas

■ Create a lampshade with a sun-printed panel, then add decorative bead trim to the edge.

SUN-PRINTED CARDS

■ Make a card by cutting up a sun print and gluing or stitching it to a blank card. Sun print rustic or handmade paper to make cards and envelopes.

■ Personalize a gift with sun-printed gift bags.

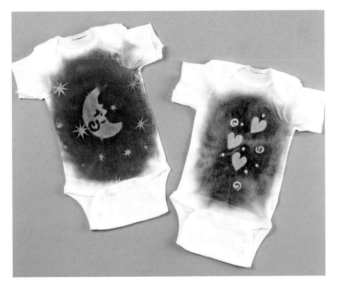

■ Need a quick shower or welcome gift for a newborn? These cute little cover-ups will take no time at all!

■ What a great host or hostess gift this apron makes. Personalize it for the recipient by sun printing pasta, flowers, and so on.

Resources

APQS: American Professional
Quilting Systems
23398 Hwy 30 East
Carroll, IA 51401
1-800-426-7233

Home of the Millennium,
Discovery, Freedom and Liberty
longarm quilt machines
www.apqs.com

Dharma Trading Company
Box 150916
San Rafael, CA 94915
1-800-542-5227

Free catalog: large selection of
paints, ready made items, clothes
blanks and related products.
www.dharmatrading.com

Dick Blick
Box 1267
Galesburg, IL 61402
1-800-447-8192

Free catalog: Large selection of art
supplies, paints and brushes.
www.dickblick.com

PRO Chemical & Dye, Inc.
Box 14
Somerset, MA 02726
1-800-228-9393

Free catalog: dyes, paints and
related products.
www.prochemical.com

Rupert, Gibbon and Spider, Inc.
P.O. Box 425
Healdsburg, CA 95448
1-800-442-0455

Fabric paints and supplies
www.jacquardproducts.com

Fire Mountain Gems & Beads
One Fire Mountain Way
Grants Pass, OR 97526-2373
1-800-423-2319

Free catalog: beads and beading
supplies
www.firmountaingems.com

Pebeo of America
1-819-829-5012
Directory for retailers of Setacolor
paints
www.pebeo.com

Michaels
63485 N Highway 97
Bend, OR 97701
1-541-312-2541

Setacolor paints, stencils, brushes,
ready made items and related items
www.michaels.com

Quilters Dream Batting
589 Central Drive
Virginia Beach, VA 23454
1-888-268-8664

Quilt batting
www.quiltersdreambatting.com

Robert Kaufmann Co.
129 W 132nd St.
Los Angeles, CA 90061
1-310-538-3482

Makers of Kona and Pimatex PFD
fabrics
www.robertkaufman.com

Robison-Anton Textile Co.
175 Bergen Blvd
Fairview, NJ 07022
1-201-941-0500

Threads for quilting and
embellishing
www.robison-anton.com

Sulky of America
P.O. Box 494129
Port Charlotte, FL 33949-4129
Fax: 941-743-4634

Threads for quilting and embellishing, stabilizers and adhesives
www.sulky.com

**For more information, ask for a
free catalog:**
C&T Publishing, Inc.
P.O. Box 1456
Lafayette, CA 94549
(800) 284-1114
Email: ctinfo@ctpub.com
www.ctpub.com

For quilting supplies:
Cotton Patch Mail Order
3405 Hall Lane, Dept.CTB
Lafayette, CA 94549
(800) 835-4418
(925) 283-7883
Email: quiltusa@yahoo.com
www.quiltusa.com

ABOUT THE AUTHORS

Barbara K. Baker

Barbara has been sewing since she was a child. Drawing was another childhood interest that occupied her time. She became interested in quilt making in the early 1970s while attending college. Finally art and sewing came together in one creative process that she has continued to explore to this day.

She teaches, designs patterns, paints on fabric, sun prints, embellishes, machine quilts, and constantly explores new possibilities in the quilting world. Purchasing an APQS longarm quilt machine expanded her horizons and expertise. Specialty threads and embellishing quilt tops take up much of her spare time. Her current passion is sun printing and embellishing each panel to create a unique work of art.

She has made quilts for Robert Kaufman Fabric Company, C&T Books and Calendars. Her work has appeared in *McCall's Quilting Magazine*, Houston Quilt Market, Spring Market, quilt shops here and in Europe. She designed the Mt. Bachelor Oregon Guild Logo and won Viewers Choice Award at the Mt. Bachelor Quilt Show.

She loves the creative process and working with colors that make her heart sing. Her quilt interests range from traditional to art quilts with brilliant colors in between. Life is too short to spend cleaning and there is always another quilt to be made, fabric to be bought, places to explore, and quilters to meet.

Jeri Boe

Jeri creates beautiful quilts and other artwork in the high desert town of Bend, Oregon. She started sewing by joining a 4-H club when she was 10, and continued sewing in 4-H until she graduated from high school. Jeri has taken tailoring and numerous art courses at the college level, and uses her painting, calligraphy, and other artistic skills when designing and making quilts, clothing, and other fun projects.

Jeri is a CPA and has a degree in Computer Information Systems. She creates hand-dyed and painted fabrics and threads and enjoys creating quilt designs and patterns. She is a passionate photographer, and often uses her photographs as inspirations for her work.

Jeri's quilts have been published in several C&T books and have appeared on calendars. Her projects have been displayed worldwide. She has taught and lectured locally, nationally, and internationally.

When Jeri is not creating quilts, she enjoys traveling and sharing the world with others. In association with Lee Greene CTA, DS, small, intimate groups are taken to fabulous locations where they explore history, culture, and art. These journeys inspire and renew her creativity, and the creativity of the group. Jeri also enjoys spending time with her husband and family. She may be found hiking, biking, snowshoeing, or rafting, often with her camera in tow just looking for the next inspiration.

Index